Better Homes and Gardens®

GREAT AMERICAN COOKOUTS

Cooking over an open fire or coals is a tradition that spans the country. For example, you can find a fish-boil cookout in the Midwest and a Spanish-style beef roast in the West. On the East Coast the New England clambake is a specialty cookout. Throughout the following pages you'll find a cross-country tour that samples outdoor cooking at its best. See how cooks of a particular region prepare food. Then, try out the recipes on your own backyard barbecue grill. Accompany the regional main-dish favorites with other tasty picnic foods and you are ready to enjoy your cookout feast.

Contents

NEW ENGLAND CLAMBAKE

When the early pilgrims arrived in America, they found Indians harvesting the sea and the land. Soon the pilgrims learned the Indian way of cooking clams in a hole with hot rocks and seaweed—an early version of a cookout. A more convenient way to enjoy a clambake cookout is to prepare the food in foil packages, then cook the bundles on a grill. For our version, two people share the contents of one package— clams, lobster tail, chicken, and corn on the cob. Serve these barbecued treats with lots of melted butter. Other accompaniments for this New England-style meal include clam chowder, rye bread, and a vegetable salad.

Clambake Bundles

8 clams in shells
2 frozen lobster tails
   (about 8 ounces each),
   thawed
1 2½- to 3-pound broiler-
   fryer chicken,
   quartered
3 tablespoons butter *or*
   margarine, melted
2 fresh ears of corn
   Rockweed *or* parsley
½ cup butter *or* margarine,
   melted

Thoroughly wash, drain, and rinse clams in salted water (⅓ cup *salt* to 1 gallon *water*) three times (let stand in the salted water 15 minutes each time). With sharp kitchen shears, cut down both sides of lobster tails; pull off thin underside membrane.

Brush chicken pieces with the 3 tablespoons melted butter or margarine. Grill the chicken over *medium-hot* coals, skin side down, for 10 minutes. Season with salt and pepper. Peel off corn husks, then remove silks from corn using a stiff brush.

Tear off four 36x18-inch pieces of heavy foil. Place 1 sheet crosswise over another sheet. Repeat to form 2 packages. Place a handful of rockweed or parsley in center of each. Cut two 18-inch squares of cheesecloth; place 1 square atop rockweed in each package. For each package, arrange the following: 4 clams, 1 lobster tail, 2 chicken quarters, and 1 ear of corn. Tie opposite ends of cheesecloth together. Seal opposite ends of foil together securely. Place on grill, seam side up, over *medium-hot* coals. Grill till chicken is done, allowing about 30 minutes on a covered grill and 35 to 40 minutes on an uncovered grill. Halve corn and lobster. Serve with individual cups of hot melted butter. Serves 4.

Marinated Vegetable Toss

1 pint fresh mushrooms,
   sliced
2 large tomatoes, chopped
½ cup sliced green onion
½ cup salad oil
½ cup dry white wine
2 tablespoons vinegar
2 teaspoons sugar
1 teaspoon dried basil,
   crushed
8 ounces fresh spinach,
   torn

In a bowl combine mushrooms, tomatoes, and green onion. In a screw-top jar combine oil, wine, vinegar, sugar, basil, and ½ teaspoon *salt*. Cover; shake well. Pour over and toss with vegetables. Cover; chill 3 to 24 hours, stirring occasionally. Before serving, drain vegetables. In a bowl toss vegetable mixture with spinach. Sieve hard-cooked egg yolks over salad, if desired. Serves 4 to 6.

Rye Bread

2 to 2½ cups all-purpose flour
¾ cup cornmeal
1 package active dry yeast
1½ cups milk
¼ cup molasses
3 tablespoons lard *or* shortening
1 teaspoon salt
1 cup rye flour

In a large mixer bowl combine *1½ cups* of the all-purpose flour, the cornmeal, and the yeast. In a saucepan heat the milk, molasses, lard or shortening, and salt just till warm (115° to 120°) and shortening is almost melted; stir constantly.

Add warm mixture to flour mixture. Beat with an electric mixer on low speed for ½ minute, scraping sides of bowl constantly. Beat for 3 minutes on high speed. Using a spoon, stir in the rye flour and as much of the remaining all-purpose flour as you can. Cover and let dough rise in a warm place till double (about 1 hour).

Stir dough down; divide in half. Place in two greased 1-quart casseroles. Cover and let rise in a warm place till nearly double (about 45 minutes). Bake in a 350° oven for 25 to 30 minutes or till bread tests done. Makes 2 loaves.

New England Clam Chowder

1 6½-ounce can minced clams
2 ounces salt pork, diced, *or* 2 slices bacon, cut up
1½ cups diced potatoes
½ cup chopped onion
1 cup milk
½ cup light cream
4 teaspoons all-purpose flour
¼ teaspoon salt
¼ teaspoon dried thyme, crushed
Dash pepper

Drain clams, reserving liquid. Add enough water to reserved liquid to measure 1 cup; set aside.

In a saucepan cook salt pork or bacon till crisp. Remove bits of pork or bacon; set aside. To the drippings in the pan add reserved clam liquid, potatoes, and onion. Cook, covered, about 15 minutes or till potatoes are tender. Stir in clams, *¾ cup* of the milk, and the cream.

Combine remaining ¼ cup milk and the flour; stir into chowder. Cook and stir till thickened and bubbly. Cook and stir 1 minute more. Stir in the salt, thyme, and pepper. To serve chowder, sprinkle the reserved salt pork or bacon atop. Makes 4 to 6 side-dish servings.

WISCONSIN FISH BOIL

Legend has it that the first fish boils were held more than a century ago by immigrants from Scandinavia who worked in the local lumber camps. Since fresh fish were available in abundance from the Great Lakes, these lumbermen found that potatoes and whitefish boiled in a huge pot outdoors made a hearty meal for the whole crew. Fish boils are often prepared in giant kettles to serve 50 or more; however, we've scaled down the fish boil recipe that follows to make six servings. Accompany the fish and potato main dish with coleslaw, a selection of breads, a chilled beverage, and pie for dessert.

Wisconsin Fish Boil

6 fresh *or* frozen whitefish
   steaks *or* other fish
   steaks (about 4 pounds)
6 to 9 medium potatoes
   (2 to 3 pounds)
16 cups hot water
¼ cup salt
½ cup butter *or* margarine,
   melted
   Lemon wedges

Thaw fish if frozen. Scrub potatoes thoroughly. Halve potatoes (leave on skin). In a heavy 8-quart kettle or Dutch oven combine water and *2 tablespoons* of the salt. Bring to boiling over *hot* coals, 35 to 40 minutes (or prepare recipe on range). Add potatoes; cook 20 to 25 minutes or till potatoes are almost tender (add more coals to fire as needed). Add fish and remaining salt to water with potatoes. Cook 7 to 8 minutes or till fish flakes easily. Skim off fish oils during cooking. Drain fish and potatoes thoroughly. Serve with melted butter and lemon wedges. Garnish with parsley, if desired. Serves 6.

Old-Fashioned Coleslaw

4 cups shredded cabbage
1 cup shredded carrot
½ cup thinly sliced celery
½ cup thinly sliced radishes
¼ cup chopped onion
½ cup mayonnaise *or* salad
   dressing
1 tablespoon sugar
1 tablespoon vinegar
½ teaspoon caraway seed
½ teaspoon celery seed

In a large bowl combine cabbage, carrot, celery, radishes, and onion. Stir together mayonnaise or salad dressing, sugar, vinegar, caraway seed, celery seed, ½ teaspoon *salt,* and dash *pepper.* Stir till sugar is dissolved. Add dressing to vegetables; toss to coat. Cover and chill. Trim salad with additional sliced radishes, if desired. Makes 6 servings.

Lemon Bread

1 egg
¾ cup milk
¼ cup cooking oil
2 teaspoons finely shredded
   lemon peel
1 tablespoon lemon juice
1¾ cups all-purpose flour
¾ cup sugar
2 teaspoons baking powder

In a mixing bowl beat together the egg, milk, oil, lemon peel, and lemon juice. Stir together flour, sugar, baking powder, and ½ teaspoon *salt.* Add to egg mixture; stir till moistened. Pour into 2 greased 6x3x2-inch loaf pans. Bake in a 350° oven for 40 to 45 minutes or till bread tests done. Cool in pans 10 minutes. Remove from pans onto wire rack. Cool. Wrap and store overnight. Makes 2 small loaves.

Pumpkin Nut Bread

1½ cups canned pumpkin
1 cup sugar
⅓ cup milk
¼ cup cooking oil
2 cups all-purpose flour
2 teaspoons baking soda
1 teaspoon ground
   cinnamon
½ teaspoon ground cloves
½ teaspoon ground ginger
½ cup chopped walnuts

In a mixing bowl stir pumpkin and sugar together. Add milk and cooking oil; mix well. Stir together flour, baking soda, cinnamon, cloves, ginger, and ½ teaspoon *salt*. Stir into pumpkin mixture. Fold in nuts. Pour into 4 greased and lightly floured 6x3x2-inch loaf pans. Bake in a 350° oven for 35 to 40 minutes or till done. Cool in pans 10 minutes. Remove from pans onto wire rack. Cool. Wrap and store overnight. Makes 4 small loaves.

Door County Cherry Pie

2 cups all-purpose flour
1 teaspoon salt
⅔ cup lard
4 to 5 tablespoons cold
   water
   Fresh Cherry Filling *or*
   Anytime Cherry Filling
1 tablespoon butter *or*
   margarine

In bowl stir together flour and salt; cut in lard till pieces are the size of small peas. Sprinkle *1 tablespoon* of the water over part of the mixture. Gently toss with fork; push to side of bowl. Repeat with remaining water till all is moistened. Form into two balls. On a floured surface roll one ball into a circle about 12 inches in diameter. Ease pastry into a 9-inch pie plate; trim pastry even with rim of pie plate. Fill pastry with desired cherry filling. Dot with butter. Roll out remaining dough; cut slits in top crust. Place pastry atop filling. Seal and flute edge high. Bake in a 375° oven for 55 to 60 minutes. Serves 8.
■ *Fresh Cherry Filling:* Combine 4 cups fresh *tart red cherries*, pitted, 1 cup *sugar*, 3 tablespoons *quick-cooking tapioca*, 1 tablespoon *cherry brandy*, 1 teaspoon finely shredded *lemon peel*, and ⅛ teaspoon *salt*. Let stand 20 minutes; stir occasionally. Do not cook.
■ *Anytime Cherry Filling:* Drain two 16-ounce cans *pitted tart red cherries*, reserving ¾ cup juice. In saucepan combine reserved cherry juice, 1 cup *sugar*, and ¼ cup *quick-cooking tapioca*. Let stand 20 minutes. Cook and stir till thickened and bubbly; cook and stir 1 minute more. Remove from heat. Stir in cherries, 1 tablespoon *cherry brandy*, 1 teaspoon finely shredded *lemon peel*, and ⅛ teaspoon *salt*.

11

TENNESSEE SMOKED PORK

Very slow, indirect cooking with hickory coals is the secret of this Southern pork barbecue. This cooking method developed from the two-pit system used in the Old South to roast a whole pig. In the original method, hickory logs were burned down to coals in one pit, then transferred to a second pit. There the hot smoke from the coals cooked the meat slowly. The meat was brushed with a sauce to keep it moist. The process took up to 24 hours, but the result made it worth the wait. Today, some Tennessee cooks use a pork shoulder and cook the meat about half that time. Our adaptation uses a covered barbecue grill with dampened hickory chips and charcoal to simulate the traditional smoke cooking.

Barbecued Pork Shoulder

Hickory chips (about
  2 pounds)
1 10- to 11-pound whole
  pork shoulder*
Tennessee Barbecue
  Sauce
10 hamburger buns

About an hour before cooking time, soak the hickory chips in enough water to cover. In a covered grill arrange *slow* coals** on both sides of a foil drip pan. Drain some of the hickory chips. Sprinkle atop coals. Trim excess fat from pork shoulder. Place shoulder, bone side down (skin side up), atop grill over drip pan. Brush with some of the Tennessee Barbecue Sauce. Lower grill hood. Grill 6 hours, adding coals and drained hickory chips as needed and brushing with sauce occasionally.

Turn shoulder; brush with additional barbecue sauce. Lower grill hood; grill 5 to 6 hours more, adding coals and hickory chips as needed and brushing with barbecue sauce. The meat should be very well done and should shred easily with a fork.

To serve, remove pork from grill. Cool slightly till meat can be handled easily. Shred meat, using two forks. Serve on hamburger buns. Heat remaining barbecue sauce and pass with sandwiches. Makes 10 to 12 servings.

*Note: If a whole pork shoulder is unavailable in your area, substitute a 5-pound pork shoulder blade Boston roast. It will serve six people. Grill it for 10 hours, 5 hours per side.

**Note: You will need about 20 pounds of charcoal to grill the meat over the long grilling time.

▪ *Tennessee Barbecue Sauce:* In a saucepan stir together 1 cup packed *brown sugar,* 1½ teaspoons *onion salt,* ½ teaspoon *paprika,* ½ teaspoon *salt,* ½ teaspoon *pepper,* and a dash *garlic salt.* Combine 2 cups *vinegar,* 1 cup bottled *barbecue sauce,* ½ cup *catsup,* 2 tablespoons *Worcestershire sauce,* and 1 tablespoon bottled *hot pepper sauce.* Stir vinegar mixture into dry ingredients. Cook and stir over low heat till sugar dissolves. Remove from heat; cool. Store, covered, in the refrigerator. Makes about 4 cups sauce.

Grandma's Potato Salad

7 medium potatoes,
   cooked, peeled, and
   coarsely chopped
   (7 cups)
3 hard-cooked eggs,
   chopped
¼ cup finely chopped sweet
   pickle
2 tablespoons chopped
   pimiento
½ cup mayonnaise
¼ cup sweet pickle juice
1 teaspoon celery seed
⅛ teaspoon garlic salt

In a large bowl combine potatoes, eggs, sweet pickle, and pimiento. Stir together mayonnaise, pickle juice, celery seed, garlic salt, 1 teaspoon *salt*, and ⅛ teaspoon *pepper*. Gently fold the mayonnaise mixture into the potato mixture. Cover and chill thoroughly. Garnish with additional hard-cooked egg slices, if desired. Makes about 10 servings.

Tangy Barbecue Slaw

¾ cup sugar
¾ cup vinegar
12 cups finely shredded
   cabbage (2½ pounds)
½ cup finely chopped onion
½ cup chopped green
   pepper
½ cup shredded carrot

In a saucepan heat together the sugar, vinegar, 1 teaspoon *salt*, and ¼ teaspoon *pepper*, stirring constantly till sugar dissolves. Cool. In a large bowl combine the shredded cabbage, onion, green pepper, and carrot. Stir dressing into the vegetable mixture. Cover. Chill several hours, stirring occasionally. Makes 10 to 12 servings.

Saucy Baked Beans

3 16-ounce cans pork and
   beans in tomato sauce
½ cup chopped onion
1 medium green pepper,
   chopped
¼ cup packed brown sugar
¼ cup catsup
2 tablespoons
   Worcestershire sauce
3 slices bacon

In a 2-quart casserole combine the pork and beans in tomato sauce, the onion, green pepper, brown sugar, catsup, and Worcestershire sauce. Top with bacon. Bake, uncovered, in a 325° oven for 1½ hours. Makes 10 to 12 servings.

TEXAS
BARBECUE

What sets a Texas barbecue apart from others is the variety and quantity of barbecued foods served. Meat combinations can include beef brisket and pork ribs as shown here, plus lots of extras. Originally, the barbecuing was done over coals in a pit dug in the ground. Today the barbecuing apparatus is more likely to be a brick-supported grill or an oversize barbecue grill. A mixture of oak and mesquite woods smokes the meat to give it a distinctive flavor, and a favorite barbecue sauce adds a "personal" touch to the meat. Other foods to round out the barbecue menu include sliced tomatoes, corn muffins, and boiled pinto beans. Also prepare your favorite potato salad recipe for this barbecue feast.

Beef Brisket Barbecue

3 to 4 cups mesquite *or*
    hickory chips
1 5- to 6-pound beef
    brisket*
    Texas Barbecue Sauce

About an hour before cooking time, soak mesquite or hickory chips in water to cover. In a covered grill arrange *hot* coals on both sides of a foil drip pan. Drain chips. Sprinkle coals with some of the chips. Place brisket atop grill over drip pan. Brush with some of the Texas Barbecue Sauce. Lower grill hood and grill 1 hour, adding coals and wood chips as needed. Turn brisket, brushing both sides with barbecue sauce. Lower hood and grill 50 to 55 minutes more or till meat is well done, adding coals and chips as needed. Brush with sauce during the last 20 minutes of cooking. Heat remaining barbecue sauce and pass with brisket**. Serves 12 to 16.

*Note: For even cooking select a beef brisket that is approximately the same thickness at both ends.

**Note: Give guests a choice of meat; refrigerate leftovers promptly. Reheat brisket for sandwiches.

■ *Texas Barbecue Sauce:* In a 1-quart saucepan combine 1 cup *tomato juice,* ¼ cup *vinegar,* ¼ cup *catsup,* ¼ cup *Worcestershire sauce,* 2 tablespoons *brown sugar,* 2 tablespoons *paprika,* 2 teaspoons *dry mustard,* 1½ teaspoons *onion salt,* ½ teaspoon *pepper,* and several dashes bottled *hot pepper sauce.* Simmer, covered, 5 minutes. Makes 2 cups sauce.

Texas Barbecued Ribs

2 cups mesquite *or* hickory
    chips
4 pounds meaty pork
    spareribs
    Texas Barbecue Sauce
    (see recipe above)

About an hour before cooking time, soak the mesquite or hickory chips in water to cover. In a covered grill arrange *hot* coals on both sides of a foil drip pan. Drain chips. Sprinkle coals with some of the chips. Place ribs atop grill over drip pan. Brush with some of the Texas Barbecue Sauce. Lower grill hood. Grill 30 minutes, adding additional coals and chips as needed. Turn ribs, brushing both sides with sauce. Lower grill hood again and grill 30 minutes more, adding chips as needed. Brush ribs with more sauce during last 20 minutes of cooking. Heat remaining sauce to pass. Serves 4 to 6.

Boiled Pinto Beans

3 cups dry pinto beans
(1¼ pounds)
8 cups cold water
5 cups water
1 teaspoon salt
1 pound ground beef
1 cup chopped onion
2 tablespoons chili powder
2 tablespoons catsup
1 teaspoon salt
¼ teaspoon pepper
Dash ground red pepper

Rinse pinto beans. In a Dutch oven or kettle combine the beans and 8 cups cold water. Bring to boiling. Reduce heat; simmer 2 minutes. Remove from heat. Cover; let stand 1 hour. (*Or,* soak beans in water overnight in a covered pan.) Drain beans and rinse. In the same Dutch oven or kettle combine rinsed beans and 5 cups more water. Add 1 teaspoon salt. Cover; heat to boiling. Reduce heat; cook over low heat for 4 hours, stirring occasionally. In skillet cook ground beef and onion till the beef is browned and the onion is tender. Drain off excess fat. Stir in chili powder, catsup, 1 teaspoon salt, the pepper, and red pepper. Stir beef mixture into beans. Cover and simmer 30 minutes, stirring occasionally. Makes 16 servings.

Chili-Cheddar Corn Muffins

2 cups yellow cornmeal
½ cup all-purpose flour
1 tablespoon baking
powder
1 tablespoon sugar
1 teaspoon baking soda
2 eggs
2½ cups milk
2 tablespoons shortening,
melted, *or* cooking oil
1 tablespoon minced dried
onion
1 cup shredded cheddar
cheese (4 ounces)
1 8¾-ounce can whole
kernel corn, drained
1 4-ounce can green chili
peppers, rinsed,
seeded, and chopped
¼ cup chopped sweet red
pepper

In a mixing bowl stir together cornmeal, flour, baking powder, sugar, baking soda, and 1¼ teaspoons *salt.* Beat together eggs, milk, melted shortening or oil, and onion. Let egg mixture stand 5 minutes to rehydrate onion. Stir into dry ingredients, beating just till smooth. Fold in cheese, *drained* corn, chili peppers, and red pepper. Spoon about *⅓ cup* batter into *each* greased and floured 2½-inch muffin cup. Bake in a 375° oven for 25 to 30 minutes. Remove from pans immediately. Makes 15 muffins.

CALIFORNIA SANTA MARIA SIRLOIN

This Spanish-style barbecue, synonymous with the city of Santa Maria, California, dates back to the early 1800s. The mainstay of the California economy then was cattle, and the annual butchering done in midsummer yielded an abundance of fresh beef. Since no way existed to store fresh meat, except by drying, everyone feasted at a large beef barbecue following every cattle roundup and ranch butchering. What was born out of necessity has become a tradition in the Santa Maria Valley and the central coastal areas of California. Although the barbecue is enjoyed backyard style by Santa Maria families, ardent barbecue chefs say that an authentic Santa Maria barbecue must feed a large group. Our family-size recipe uses a beef top sirloin.

Santa Maria Barbecued Sirloin

Red oak logs *or* charcoal
    and oak chips
1 tablespoon salt
½ teaspoon garlic salt
½ teaspoon pepper
1 3- to 4-pound boneless
    beef top sirloin, cut 3
    inches thick
Salsa (see recipe below)

Prepare fire in barbecue unit using red oak logs or a combination of charcoal and oak chips. Allow logs or charcoal to burn down to red coals. Combine salt, garlic salt, and pepper; shake or rub over surface of meat. Place meat on grill grate and lower grate to within 2 to 3 inches from *hot* coals. Sear underside of meat 5 to 10 minutes to seal in juices, then raise grate till meat is 6 to 8 inches above coals. Continue cooking* 20 minutes. Turn meat; lower grate to sear other side. Raise again and continue cooking 20 to 30 minutes longer or till meat is desired doneness. Slice the meat and serve with Salsa. Makes 6 to 8 servings.

*Note: Do not let coals flame up. Use a spray bottle of water to keep flames down.

Salsa

3 fresh medium tomatoes,
    chopped
½ cup chopped green onion
½ cup finely chopped celery
1 4-ounce can green chili
    peppers, rinsed,
    seeded, and
    chopped
2 tablespoons cilantro *or*
    parsley
1 tablespoon vinegar
2 teaspoons Worcestershire
    sauce
½ teaspoon garlic salt
½ teaspoon dried oregano,
    crushed
Few drops bottled hot
    pepper sauce

In a bowl combine tomatoes, green onion, celery, chili peppers, cilantro or parsley, vinegar, Worcestershire sauce, garlic salt, oregano, and bottled hot pepper sauce. Cover and let stand at least 1 hour to blend flavors. Makes 3½ cups sauce.

Pinquito Barbecue Beans

1 pound pinquito beans,
      pink beans, *or* pinto
      beans
10 cups cold water
8 cups water
½ teaspoon salt
6 ounces bacon, diced
      (6 or 7 slices)
1 medium onion, chopped
      (½ cup)
1 stalk celery, chopped
      (½ cup)
1 clove garlic, minced
4 ounces ground fully
      cooked ham
½ cup tomato puree
¼ cup chili sauce
2 tablespoons sugar
1 tablespoon dry mustard
1 tablespoon vinegar
2 teaspoons salt
½ teaspoon pepper

Rinse beans. In a Dutch oven or kettle combine the beans and the 10 cups cold water. Bring to boiling. Reduce heat; simmer 2 minutes. Remove from heat. Cover and let stand 1 hour. (*Or,* soak beans in water overnight in a covered pan.) Drain beans and rinse. In the same Dutch oven or kettle combine the rinsed beans and the 8 cups water. Add the ½ teaspoon salt to beans and water; cover. Simmer beans 2½ to 3 hours or till tender. (Cook pinto beans 1½ to 2 hours.) Drain the beans, reserving 3½ cups liquid. Return beans and the 3½ cups liquid to Dutch oven.

In a skillet cook bacon till lightly browned; drain off excess fat. Add onion, celery, and garlic. Cook vegetables 10 minutes or till tender. Add ham, tomato puree, chili sauce, sugar, dry mustard, vinegar, the 2 teaspoons salt, and pepper; stir till sugar is dissolved. Bring to boiling. Stir vegetable mixture into beans. Simmer, uncovered, for 45 minutes, stirring occasionally. Makes 6 to 8 servings.

Macaroni and Cheese

1½ cups elbow macaroni
2 tablespoons butter *or*
      margarine
2 tablespoons all-purpose
      flour
¾ teaspoon salt
   Dash pepper
2 cups milk
1½ cups shredded sharp
      cheddar cheese
      (6 ounces)

Cook macaroni according to package directions; drain. In a saucepan melt butter or margarine; stir in the flour, salt, and pepper. Add milk all at once. Cook and stir till thickened and bubbly. Stir in *1 cup* of the cheese till melted. Combine macaroni and cheese sauce. Turn into a 1½-quart casserole. Sprinkle with the remaining ½ cup cheese. Bake in a 350° oven for 30 minutes. Makes 6 to 8 servings.

Index